PRINCE PHILIP

Duke of Edinburgh

PRINCE PHILIP

Duke of Edinburgh

ANNIE BULLEN

Previous page right: Prince Philip arrives at Royal Ascot in June 2007.
Previous page left: Navy 'whites' are worn by Prince Philip during the Royal Salute at Kiribati on a tour of Australia and the South Pacific in October 1982.

Publication in this form copyright © Pitkin Publishing 2017.
Text © Pitkin Publishing 2017.

Written by Annie Bullen.
The moral right of the author has been asserted.

Edited by Gill Knappett and Halima Sadat.
Picture research by Gill Knappett.
Design by Lee-May Lim and Katie Beard.

All photographs by kind permission of Press Association Images and Mary Evans except for
Select bibliography:
Philip and Elizabeth: Portrait of a Marriage by Gyles Brandreth (Century, 2004)
Young Prince Philip: His Turbulent Early Life by Philip Eade (HarperPress, 2012)

Published by Pitkin Publishing, Pavilion Books Company Limited
43 Great Ormond Street, London WC1N 3HZ, UK
Sales and enquiries: +44 (0)20 7462 1506
Email: sales@pavilionbooks.com

Printed in Turkey.
ISBN: 978-1-84165-783-7

CONTENTS

A MOMENTOUS MEETING

The Royal Yacht *Victoria and Albert* made stately progress along the Devon coast in late July 1939. On board were King George VI, his wife, Queen Elizabeth, and their two daughters, 13-year-old Princess Elizabeth and her younger sister, Princess Margaret Rose.

The sisters, happy to be reunited with their parents, newly returned from a triumphant tour of North America, were enjoying this excursion to the Royal Naval College at Dartmouth, where the King, who had been a cadet there a quarter of a century earlier, was to undertake an inspection. The weekend weather was warm and sunny, belying the dark clouds of war that were gathering over Europe.

On board too, attending the royal family to whom he was related, was Lord Louis Mountbatten. With him was his nephew, Prince Philip of Greece, a Special Entry recruit into the Royal Navy who was being fast-tracked through Dartmouth on a three-month initial officers' training course. Philip, just turned 18, tall and handsome with blond hair and bright blue eyes, entertaining and personable, was invited for dinner on Saturday 22 July. The Princesses, looked after by their governess, had their supper in the nursery. But the following day Philip was detailed to entertain his young cousins when it was revealed that mumps and chickenpox in the college prevented the Princesses from attending a planned service in the chapel.

They played with a train set before Philip, becoming bored, encouraged the sisters into the grounds where he impressed the girls by showing his prowess at jumping tennis nets

Right: The Royal Yacht *Victoria and Albert,* with the young Princess Elizabeth on board, steams towards the Royal Naval College, Dartmouth, on 22 July 1939.

Left: Their first meeting at Dartmouth Royal Naval College: the 13-year-old Princess Elizabeth sits towards the far left of the photograph, while her future husband, Prince Philip of Greece, in a white-topped cap, is seen laughing and chatting at the back.

before setting up a game of croquet. Elizabeth, 'Lilibet' to her family and friends, was dressed identically to Margaret, both wearing neat double-breasted light coats, knee-length white socks, sensible shoes and berets. Just in her teens, slight and slim, Elizabeth was still childlike. But that meeting was one she did not forget and, when the royal party set sail, the young Princess picked up a pair of field glasses to watch Philip as he valiantly rowed in their wake until they left him far behind.

It is likely that Princess Elizabeth, then heir presumptive to the British throne, knew of her cousin's turbulent and often sad family background. It is likely that, protected by nannies, her governess and by the rigid protocol that surrounded her family, she found Philip an exciting and romantic figure. It is thought by many that the 13-year-old fell in love that weekend and set her sights unswervingly on the man who was to become her husband and lifelong companion in one of the most remarkable partnerships in the history of the British monarchy.

At 18, Philip, an able and talented young man, had a promising naval career ahead, accelerated by the fast-approaching war. He left Dartmouth with the King's Dirk, the prize for the best all-round cadet of his intake. Family circumstances meant that he was virtually homeless, living at boarding school or with his grandmother, Princess Victoria of Hesse, Marchioness of Milford Haven, or with one of his English uncles. He was self-reliant, a leader and a man able to deal with whatever life threw his way. But when Princess Elizabeth, who became his wife in 1947, acceded to the British throne early in 1952, he provided the support that she needed, giving up any hopes he might have had of a separate career. In doing so he still remained his own man, acting in his own inimitable way as an ambassador for Britain, a forthright participant in the daily rota of visits, engagements and ritual that is the lot of senior members of the royal family.

Below: Young and handsome: 18-year-old Prince Philip.

FAMILY
BACKGROUND

Queen Victoria was great-great-grandmother to both Queen Elizabeth and Prince Philip, each being born after her death in 1901. But although they had an illustrious ancestor in common, their upbringing could not have been more different.

Elizabeth was the beloved elder daughter of the Duke of York who, at the time of her birth, had no idea that he would become King. He was the younger son of King George V. His 'Lilibet' became the King's first granddaughter. Her childhood was secure, comfortable and cosseted.

Philip was born on 10 June 1921 on the dining table of his parents' villa, *Mon Repos*, on the island of Corfu. His father, a prince and a soldier, was commanding the Greek army's 12th division in Asia Minor and did not see his son until three months after his birth. His mother, Princess Alice, and his four older sisters lived in the house which had been left to the family by his paternal grandfather, George I of Greece, who had been assassinated in March 1913. Philip's uncle, Constantine I, who assumed the Greek crown during the first Balkan War, suffered exile, as did his father, Andrea. Another uncle, Alexander, who briefly took the crown during Constantine's exile, was bitten by a monkey and died of blood poisoning. His Russian relations had been murdered in 1918. Philip was barely a year old when his father narrowly escaped being sentenced to death by the new republican Greek government. He and his family fled their villa in Corfu into exile.

They settled, eventually, in Paris where they lived at St Cloud in the lodge of the substantial house of Andrea's elder brother, Prince George (known to the family as 'Big George'), who was married to the wealthy Marie Bonaparte. By the time Philip was nine, his mother had become ill and had been taken to a Swiss psychiatric sanatorium. Philip had already been sent to Cheam, an English preparatory school, his father had moved to a small flat in Monte Carlo, while his four sisters had married and moved away. The family had broken apart.

Although Prince Philip was, briefly, sixth in line to the Greek throne, he has no Greek blood; in fact he descends from a Danish family. His grandfather, King George I of Greece, was born Prince William of Schleswig-Holstein-Sonderburg-Glücksburg in 1845 in Copenhagen. Suddenly, Prince William's

Below: Queen Victoria smiles at baby Alice (later Prince Philip's mother). Alice is held by Princess Victoria of Hesse, the Queen's granddaughter. Also in the picture is Princess Beatrice, aunt to the younger Victoria and daughter of the Queen.

Left: Princess Elizabeth was christened at the private chapel at Buckingham Palace in May 1926. Here she is held by her mother, the Duchess of York, who is seated next to Queen Mary. Standing behind them are King George V and the Duke of York.

Below: Philip's family in 1906, 15 years before his birth. His grandmother, Princess Victoria of Hesse, holds his sisters Margarita and Theodora; seated on the right is Alice, Philip's mother (Princess Victoria's daughter); seated on the left is Alice's sister Louise, at the time Queen of Sweden. Standing on the left is Prince Louis of Battenberg, Victoria's husband, and next to him is his son-in-law, Prince Andrew of Greece, father to Philip and his sisters. Sitting at the front are Victoria's two younger children (Philip's uncles), Louis and George Mountbatten.

father became King Christian IX of Denmark and a delegation arrived from Greece to ask William to become their king. William, just 17 and now King George I, arrived in Athens, having given up a naval career to rule a turbulent people in a distant land. He married a Russian noblewoman, Olga, niece of Tsar Alexander II. They had eight children (one of whom, baby Olga, survived just seven months), the last but one being Andrew, known always as Andrea, Prince Philip's father.

Philip's mother, Alice, was the daughter of Queen Victoria's granddaughter, Princess Victoria, who married the larger-than-life Prince Louis of Battenberg. He went on to become First Sea Lord and 1st Marquess of Milford Haven and with Victoria, he produced four children. The eldest, Alice, Philip's mother, despite being born deaf, was noted for her beauty, poise and cleverness. Their youngest son, also Louis but known as 'Dickie', became Admiral of the Fleet, Earl Mountbatten of Burma.

Andrea met his future wife in 1902 when both were guests at the coronation of King Edward VII, which had been delayed because of the King's sudden appendicitis. The young couple fell in love and became engaged.

In May 1903, King Edward VII, now safely crowned and recovered from his appendectomy, agreed that Alice and Andrea should be married. The wedding took place five months later at the Hesse family home, Darmstadt, just south of Frankfurt. It was a magnificent affair lasting two days, with guests from many royal families, including Andrea's cousin, Tsar Nicholas II, son of his aunt Dagmar. The Tsar's wife, Alix, was Alice's aunt.

Alice, not yet out of her teens, was welcomed warmly into her bridegroom's family home in Athens and the first 10 years of her married life saw the birth of three daughters: Margarita, Theodora and Cecile, Prince Philip's older sisters. This was a troubled time in Greek politics, culminating in the onset of the Balkan Wars in 1912. Alice, while still enjoying family life at home with her daughters and travelling widely to England, Germany and Russia on family visits and to attend christenings, weddings and funerals, also became deeply involved in serving her new people. She started by organising the mass fabrication of warm clothes for the Greek troops, setting the pupils at the Greek School of Embroidery the task of making thousands of jackets and hoods for the fighting men.

Her husband, Andrea, a lieutenant-colonel in the Greek army, was posted to Larissa on the former Turkish border. Alice went with him and was appalled by the awful sights of war and the lack of facilities to care for the wounded brought back from the front. She set to commandeering buildings and vehicles, organising doctors and nurses and founding field hospitals, rolling up her sleeves and helping the nursing staff and doctors, doing all she could to tend the wounded and care for the dying. Alice did not falter at the sight of bloody heads and shattered limbs; she assisted at amputations and became adept at bandaging the terrible wounds. Her three young daughters stayed behind in Athens with their grandparents.

Below: Prince Andrew of Greece, Philip's father, in 1913.

Above left: Princess Alice of Greece, Philip's mother, in 1913.

Above right: Philip's four older sisters in about 1915: left to right are the Princesses Theodora, Sophie (the baby), Margarita and Cecile.

In 1913, the second Balkan War ended, with Greece gaining an enormous amount of territory; Alice received the Royal Red Cross from King George V of the United Kingdom 'in recognition of her services … during the recent war'. But the ever-present worry of a much larger conflict loomed over the whole of Europe.

The Greek royal family was mourning the loss of King George I, who, approaching his Golden Jubilee on the Greek throne, had announced in March 1913 that he intended to abdicate in October that year. He was in Salonika when he made the announcement, at the lunch table. Later that afternoon, as he was strolling in the streets, a man rushed out of a café and shot him dead. He was succeeded by his eldest son, Constantine, Andrea's brother.

Both Constantine and Andrea (whose last daughter, Sophie, was born in 1914) found themselves in uncomfortable territory when war broke out in 1914. The new king's wife, also called Sophie, was the sister of Kaiser Wilhelm II. Alice, born a German princess, was in a similarly difficult situation. Constantine decided to stay neutral in the war, which was not a popular move with the British.

Alice's father, Louis of Battenberg, the indubitably loyal and shrewd First Sea Lord of Britain, had served for more than 40 years in the British Navy, yet anti-German propaganda and paranoia eventually forced his resignation in October 1914, a move deeply resented by his wife, Queen Victoria's granddaughter. A few years later his title was changed from His Serene Highness Prince Louis of Battenberg to the Marquess of Milford Haven and his family name 'Battenberg' was anglicised to 'Mountbatten'.

Louis's son, 'Dickie', Alice's younger brother, then a naval cadet, was to avenge his father's downfall.

A BOY IS BORN

In June 1917, four years before Prince Philip's birth, the Greek royal family was at odds with the Allies as they continued to insist on the nation's neutrality. The Greek prime minister, Eleftherios Venizelos, had other ideas and established a rival government which declared war on Germany. Eventually Constantine was exiled to Switzerland where he was joined by Andrea and Alice and their four daughters. Constantine was replaced by his second son, who became King Alexander for a mere three years, dying at the royal family's country home at Tatoi in the foothills of Mount Parnés. His death in 1920 was extraordinarily unlucky – he was walking in the grounds when a pair of monkeys attacked his dog. Alexander was bitten on the leg as he tried to beat them off and died three weeks later of blood poisoning.

Prime Minister Venizelos offered the Greek people the right to vote for the restoration of the throne to the exiled King Constantine. To the amazement of all, the vote was decisive. Venizelos and his government were swept from office and Constantine returned to Greece. With him were Andrea and Alice – now pregnant with her fifth child.

Andrea, made major-general, returned to his army duties in Athens. Alice, expecting her baby in June 1921, went to their villa, *Mon Repos*, on the sunny island of Corfu, where she and her daughters were looked after by a small retinue of servants, which included an English housekeeper as well as handyman, and Alice's elderly nanny, Miss Emily Roose. The villa, left to Philip's parents by Andrea's father, King George, had no modern comforts

Right: A happy baby: Philip at 14 months.

Far right: The young Prince Philip, aged about four, enjoying himself on a beach with his parents, Prince and Princess Andrew of Greece.

While Philip's parents suffered exile and his grandfather underwent a change of name and was forced into retirement from a job he loved, the fate of his Russian relatives was terrible. The Romanovs, his father's cousin, Tsar Nicholas, and his mother's, aunt Tsarina Alix, were taken, with their five children, to a hideaway in the Ural mountains where they were eventually shot with their servants. Alice's other aunt, Ella, married to a Russian Grand Duke and known for her good works, was arrested by secret police and, along with other members of the imperial family, was blindfolded and shackled before being hurled alive down a mineshaft. It is said that when they were heard singing hymns and praying, grenades were thrown into the shaft to ensure that they died.

such as electricity or running hot water but it was secluded and in a beautiful position, looking over the Ionian Sea.

On 9 June, Andrea, at last given the command of a division, left Athens for Smyrna, to lead troops in the ongoing Turkish campaign. Early on the morning of the following day, 10 June, Alice, now 36 years old, went into labour and was helped onto the villa's dining-room table by the local doctor who decided this was the best place for her to give birth. A baby boy, later registered as Philippos, was delivered at 10am. The child was sixth in line to the Greek throne.

Alice wrote to her family at Darmstadt that her new baby, a boy at last, was 'a splendid healthy child'. She confirmed that she had had an easy delivery and was enjoying the pleasant sea air from her chaise longue on the terrace. Blond-haired, blue-eyed Philip was the darling of a household full of women. He was a chubby, happy baby, the longed-for boy of the family.

Sadly Philip's only living grandfather, Louis, now Marquess of Milford Haven, died in September at the age of 67. Alice came to London to be with her mother, bringing Philip with her.

EARLY DAYS –
AND EXILE

The three-month-old Philip was cuddled and kissed by assorted aunts and uncles at Osborne House on the Isle of Wight, where his grandfather was taken for burial. The baby's uncle, Dickie Mountbatten, unaware of the part he would play in his nephew's future, was one of these fond relatives.

To Alice's surprise, Andrea was waiting at their villa when she and their baby son returned home to Corfu. It was Andrea's first sight of Philip and, despondent as he was with the way the military campaign in Asia Minor was being conducted, his spirits must have lifted as he held the child in his arms.

He was back at home, too, in the spring of 1922, on his way to a posting in the northwest of the country, when Alice's mother, Victoria, and sister, Louise, came to stay. Philip, aged just 11 months, was already crawling and standing up. Victoria reported that her young grandson was the image of his father. Louise commented that he laughed all day and that she had never seen such a cheerful baby.

Alice and her children travelled to London just after Philip's first birthday to attend the magnificent wedding of her brother, Dickie Mountbatten, to heiress Edwina Ashley. The wedding, at St Margaret's Westminster on 18 July, was the event of the season. Alice's four daughters were bridesmaids while the best man was the Prince of Wales. Little Philip was left behind in the care of nannies at Spencer House, in St James's, London.

Right: Osborne House, Queen Victoria's home on the Isle of Wight, where Prince Philip's grandfather is buried.

While the family was still enjoying reunions in London, more than 30,000 Greek and Armenian Christians were massacred in Smyrna by Turkish forces. A million more escaped and the remnants of the Greek army withdrew to the coast. Greece was humiliated; King Constantine abdicated and fled into exile while the new government looked for those responsible for this military disaster – among them Philip's father, who was taken from Corfu and imprisoned in Athens. By this time, Alice and the children were back home with no idea when he would return.

The first group of those deemed to be responsible for the military debacle were subject to court-martial, all charged with high treason for allowing enemy troops onto Greek territory. All were found guilty, six sentenced to death and two to life imprisonment. Andrea was due to face a court-martial soon after the executions and his prospects did not look good. But he was the cousin of George V of Great Britain and behind-the-scenes negotiations took place to ensure that he would escape with his life.

On Saturday 2 December, Andrea was found guilty of disobeying an order and abandoning his post in the face of an enemy. He was banished from Greece for life. The following day he was taken quietly to the quay at Phaleron where the British cruiser *Calypso* waited. Alice was already aboard. *Calypso* slipped mooring en route for southern Italy via Corfu, where nanny Emily Roose, three other servants and the five children were picked up. Philip's sisters had hastily packed essential possessions and had lit every fire in the house to burn letters, papers and documents before being taken hurriedly by car and small boat out to the cruiser waiting offshore for their embarkation.

Philip, just 18 months old, of course remembered nothing of the escape, during which he slept on board in a crib made from a roughly converted fruit crate. On arrival at Brindisi, the family travelled by train to Rome and then on to France where they stayed in a Paris hotel while they tried to sort out where and how they were to live.

Above right: Philip's uncle, Lord Louis Mountbatten, and Edwina Ashley on their wedding day, 18 July 1922.

Right: Philip with his mother in January 1924, after the family fled into exile.

SCHOOL DAYS AND HOLIDAYS

Once Greece was declared a republic in 1924 and all hope of return was gone, the exiled family made their home at St Cloud on the western outskirts of Paris. Relatives lived nearby and visits to other family members throughout Europe were frequent. Philip was surrounded by adults who adored him. On holiday in Bordeaux in 1923, his mother's sister, Philip's Aunt Louise, wrote that he was a 'perfect pet' and 'the sturdiest little boy I have seen'.

He visited London the following year and was excited, so Alice recorded, to see buses and policemen. Frequent visits were made to the farm near Marseilles where the Foufounis family, loyal Greek royalists, lived. Their three children and Philip became close, while Madame Foufounis once confessed that she loved the boy as her own.

He would also stay with relatives at Panker, a castle on the Baltic coast, where he and his cousins played for hours on the beach, shrimping and splashing in the sea. Sometimes he and his sisters spent time with their cousin, Helen, daughter of the late King Constantine and estranged wife of King Carol of Romania. There they played with Helen's son, Michael, who was only five years old when he became King of Romania under a regency.

Right: A happy young Philip (standing on the far left) with classmates at the MacJannet American School in the Paris suburb of St Cloud.

Philip was six when Alice arranged for him to start at his first school, the Elms, which occupied Jules Verne's old home at St Cloud, just above the River Seine. Alice told the headmaster that her son should learn to speak good English as she envisaged him eventually living in England or America. She also wanted the Anglo-Saxon ideals of courage and fair play instilled in her boy. At the time, the family spoke English at home, but conversation would veer into other European languages, including French, Greek and German.

Until this time, Alice was fully involved with Philip's upbringing, but it was becoming increasingly obvious that she was not well and that her relationship with Andrea suffered as a result. Her illness was mental rather than physical, although her bodily health was affected by her obsession with messages from the spirit world and various delusions. A short stay in a Berlin clinic was eventually followed by her committal, in May 1930, to the Bellevue sanatorium at Kreuzlingen on the shores of Lake Constance. This was the point at which close family life was over for Philip. Andrea left St Cloud for Monte Carlo, passing Philip into the care of his grandmother, Victoria, and his uncles, the Mountbattens. His sisters were all on the point of leaving home – each of them married within a couple of years of the family falling apart. Victoria had become increasingly involved in her grandson's upbringing as his mother's mental health deteriorated and she initially looked after him in her apartment at Kensington Palace. But there was little to entertain a small boy and Philip's great-aunt, Princess Beatrice, Queen Victoria's younger daughter, also ensconced at Kensington Palace, was distinctly not amused by the disturbance to her life.

And so Alice's elder brother, Georgie, now the second Marquess of Milford Haven, became Philip's guardian at his home, Lynden Manor, Holyport, near Maidenhead on the River Thames. Philip joined Georgie's son, David, at Cheam, Britain's oldest prep school, then situated at Tabor Court in Surrey. Philip adapted quickly to school life, despite the fact that his French was better than his English and he seemed different from the other boys, unused as he was to the English way of life. But this little boy, with white-blond hair and quiet self-possession, was extremely good at games and this won him acceptance in no time at all.

Above: Philip (left) rides out with his cousin, Prince Michael of Romania, at Constanza in August 1928.

Left: Philip's uncle, George Battenberg, in uniform in 1929. He took on the guardianship of Prince Philip when the young boy's mother became unwell.

GORDONSTOUN

It is well documented that Philip's secondary education took place at Gordonstoun in remote Scottish countryside near the Moray Firth. What is not so well known is that he left Cheam in 1933 – the year Hitler became German Chancellor – to study at the German school, Salem, which occupied part of an enormous castle near Lake Constance, belonging to the father-in-law of Theodora, Philip's second sister.

When it was founded in 1920, by a remarkable man called Kurt Hahn, who believed that young people should be given the space and freedom to discover what they are capable of achieving, Salem was acknowledged as a progressive and liberal establishment. But by the time Philip arrived at the school, its headmaster, Hahn, had been arrested by the Gestapo after he had told the boys they must choose between the humanitarian values of Salem and those of the Nazis. The Salem Philip joined was already seeing the influence of the new regime with its military athletics and endless drilling. Although Philip lived with his sister while he attended the school, he never felt properly integrated and found the drilling, foot-slogging and the introduction of the Nazi salute tedious and ridiculous. It was with relief that he learnt that his father had decided he should return to England to attend another school founded by Kurt Hahn – Gordonstoun.

Hahn had fled Germany in 1932 with the help of the British Prime Minister Ramsay MacDonald, and with the encouragement of leading educationists and academics, eventually leased Gordonstoun House and 300 acres (120ha) of rugged land on the Morayshire coast, opening his new school with just 13 pupils two years later.

When Philip arrived in the autumn of 1934, numbers had increased to 27 and, because of the spartan and neglected nature of the buildings and estate, the boys were expected to help on the farm, in the gardens and house, and even in the construction and decoration

Below left: Gordonstoun School, Elgin, in the early 1950s.

Below right: Philip at Gordonstoun with the school cricket team in 1935. He is in the centre with the cricket ball.

of classrooms. Comfortable it was not, but Gordonstoun was certainly exciting, pioneering and character-building.

The boys took a bracing cold shower at 6.30am before going for a run. Lessons after breakfast were followed by a spot of jumping and javelin-throwing. The boys lay on their backs after lunch, resting, while a teacher read to them; in the afternoons they played games twice a week (but no more), carried out a 'common task' or worked on a project such as music, art, gardening or building. On two afternoons they studied seamanship, learning to sail at nearby Hopeman, an act that triggered the beginning of Philip's lifelong love of the sea and ships.

The young Philip, just 13, responded to the environment, eventually developing respect for his school and his eccentric headmaster. Hahn reciprocated, writing a piece for Reuters news agency in 1947, emphasising Philip's 'undefeatable spirit'. 'He felt deeply both joy and sadness, and the way he looked and the way he moved, indicated what he felt ... But for the most part he enjoyed his life, his laughter was heard everywhere and created merriness around him,' wrote Hahn.

Above: The Duke of Edinburgh meets his old Gordonstoun headmaster, Kurt Hahn, in 1964.

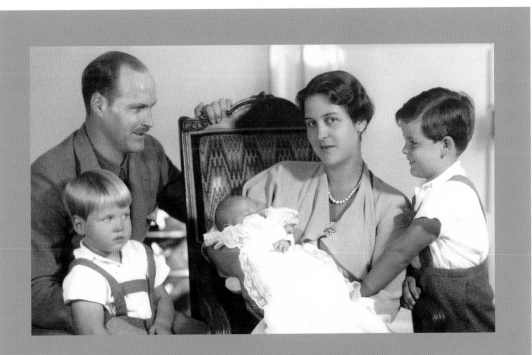

Left: Philip's sister, Cecile, with her husband, Prince Georg Donatus of Hesse, and their children, Ludwig, Alexander and baby Johanna, in 1936. Tragically, the whole family, except for Johanna, was killed in a plane crash in 1937. Johanna died of meningitis in 1939.

Sadness marred Philip's time at Gordonstoun when, in November 1937, it fell to headmaster Kurt Hahn to tell him of the death of his sister Cecile, her husband the Grand Duke of Hesse, their two young sons and her unborn child in an air crash at Ostend as they were travelling to London for a family wedding. Philip travelled alone to Darmstadt, the Hesse family home near Frankfurt, for the funeral, where he walked behind the coffins, his ash-blond hair standing out against his dark coat. This deeply sad occasion was the first time he had seen his mother and father together since the family split apart in 1931.

INTO THE
ROYAL NAVY

Family sadnesses and tragedy punctuated Philip's last year at Gordonstoun but, at 16, tempered by the turmoil and disruption he had already experienced in his young life, he coped quietly with the deaths of his sister and her family in the 1937 air crash. He was clearly deeply affected by the terrible loss, but his headmaster wrote, 'his sorrow was that of a man'.

Another blow fell the following year, in April 1938, when his guardian and uncle, Georgie Milford Haven, died of bone-marrow cancer. The Milford Havens had provided Philip with a home and stability. Now Georgie's younger brother, Dickie Mountbatten, stepped forward to act as his guardian and mentor.

Philip left Gordonstoun in 1939, having spent his last term there as 'guardian' or head boy. He had been captain of cricket and his final report from headmaster Hahn praised his 'public spirit' as 'exemplary', his sense of justice as 'never failing' and extolled his 'natural power of command'. Hahn wrote that Philip was a 'born leader' but warned that he would need the 'exacting demands of great service to do justice to himself ...'.

It is documented that the young Philip's desire was to become a fighter pilot, but his love of ships and sailing, inculcated by the regime at Gordonstoun and by the influence of his uncle Dickie, whose own naval career had been meteoric, steered him towards a life at sea. His grandfather, Prince Louis of Battenberg, had, after all, been First Sea Lord and family tradition dictated that he enter the senior service. There had been some debate whether he should join the navy of Greece, the country of his birth, but by early 1938 he was studying hard for his entrance exams for the Royal Navy in Britain which, increasingly, was becoming home.

Left: Lord Louis ('Dickie') Mountbatten, and his wife, Edwina, in Florida in 1938. After the death of Philip's guardian, Uncle Georgie, the couple welcomed the young man into their home.

Left: Dartmouth
Royal Naval College.

He began to stay often with his uncle at Adsdean, the Mountbattens' grand country home near Portsmouth, where they lived until Dickie's wife, Edwina, inherited Broadlands in Hampshire. At Adsdean he could enjoy the polo practice field, golf course and tennis courts and almost 1,000 acres (400ha) of shooting. But Philip, keen to achieve his goal of a career at sea, kept his head down and studied. Mountbatten arranged for him to stay for a while with a naval coach at Cheltenham, Gloucestershire, in order to prepare for entry to Dartmouth Royal Naval College. He eventually came a credible 16th out of the 34 young men who were admitted to Dartmouth in that intake. He entered the college in May 1939 as a special cadet, spending two terms on land and two in the training cruiser. It was in late July that he was invited on board the Royal Yacht *Victoria and Albert (see pages 6–7)* and helped to entertain the two young Princesses, Elizabeth and Margaret.

Below: A bearded
Philip, during a
naval visit to
Melbourne,
Australia, in
August 1945.

But all was not well in the wider world. War in Europe was inevitable and when the declaration came on 3 September 1939, Philip, still a prince of Greece, was actually staying in the land of his birth, where, in 1935, the monarchy had been restored. He was on holiday there with his mother, Alice, now apparently recovered from the mental trauma that had taken her away from her family for so many years. His mother and grandmother felt he should stay in Greece, but Philip, torn, wanted to finish his naval training and fight for England. His cousin, King George II of Greece, helped him make up his mind, telling him that it would be sensible to return to Britain to continue at Dartmouth.

AN AUSPICIOUS WAR

The King's Dirk and the Eardley-Howard-Crockett prize for top performances at Dartmouth were Philip's as he left Dartmouth Naval College, but his future at sea was still uncertain. The problem was that as a citizen of Greece, a neutral country, he was barred from wartime service. Eventually it was decided he could join HMS *Ramillies*, an outdated battleship escorting convoys of Australian and New Zealand troopships bound for Egypt. Midshipman Philip of Greece cheerfully put up with the sweltering heat below decks and his role as a general dogsbody, although he was longing to see some real action.

Just as he was becoming accustomed to the routine on *Ramillies*, he was transferred to the County class cruiser *Kent*, where he found the ventilation better and was able to sleep in comfort. Their route, escorting British troops from Bombay to Britain round the Cape of Good Hope, gave them a week's much-appreciated relaxation in Durban. Then came a spell on *Kent*'s sister ship *Shropshire*, before Italy joined the war and made a move that propelled Philip into the action. Mussolini, hoping to impress Hitler, torpedoed a Greek light cruiser before invading Greece from Albania. Greece sided with the Allied Forces and Philip, a Greek citizen, was able to take a more active part in the fighting. He travelled to Alexandria, where he joined the battleship *Valiant*, part of the Mediterranean Fleet, and was soon in the thick of the bombardment of Bardia on the Libyan coast and then on to

Below: Philip, in naval uniform, in December 1946.

Below right: The battleship *Valiant* in March 1945.

Sicily, where he witnessed the loss of the destroyer *Southampton*.

In 1941, Philip was to play a key part in a dramatic night battle to foil the Italian fleet which, codebreakers had learnt, was threatening an Allied convoy to Greece. As darkness fell on the night of 27 March, *Valiant* quietly left Alexandria, following the *Warsprite*, Admiral Andrew Cunningham's flagship. With them was the aircraft carrier *Formidable*, the *Barham* and nine destroyers. They came across the Italian ships southwest of Cape Matapan and engaged in long-range fire. Two Italian ships were severely damaged and Cunningham decided to wait for darkness, relying on British night-fighting skills to inflict further damage. *Valiant* and *Barham* opened fire at close range in the dark and three heavy cruisers and two destroyers belonging to the Italian fleet were sunk. Philip's role had been to operate the *Valiant*'s searchlights so that the gunners could do their job. For this he was mentioned in Admiral Cunningham's dispatches and awarded the Greek War Cross.

Two months later, *Valiant* was off Crete, as part of a greater force trying to intercept German landings on the island, when she was damaged by enemy bombers.

Above: The Duke of Edinburgh transfers ships during exercises in the Mediterranean in April 1955.

During the action Philip sat his sub-lieutenant's examination, comprising gunnery, torpedoes, navigation, signals and seamanship, passing with a top ('one') grade in four of the subjects and a 'two' in the other.

In June 1942, he was posted to the *Wallace* at Rosyth on escort duty on the treacherous 60-hour journey to Sheerness, on the Kent coast, under threat from German E-boats and bombers. In October that year, his captain requested that he be made first lieutenant, second-in-command of the ship. At just 21 years old, he was one of the youngest men in the Royal Navy to hold that position.

It is reported that Philip and Elizabeth wrote 'cousinly' letters to each other throughout the war and, in October 1941, the young sailor spent his leave at Windsor Castle, where he talked of his Mediterranean exploits. Later, King George VI wrote to Victoria, Philip's grandmother, 'What a charming boy he is, and I am glad he is remaining on in my Navy.'

A SECRET
ENGAGEMENT

Christmas 1943 saw Philip invited to Windsor Castle and to the annual royal panto in which the Princesses Elizabeth and Margaret were to play the leading roles. Elizabeth, according to her governess Marion Crawford, was animated and excited at the prospect of seeing her handsome cousin. Sadly Philip went down with flu and missed the opening night of the show, only recovering in time to see the third performance, just a week before Christmas. He joined the Christmas party at Windsor, enjoying family festivities which included a film, dinner parties, charades and rolling back the carpet to dance in the Crimson Drawing Room until well past midnight on Boxing Day.

His presence there, reported in the newspapers, fuelled rumours that romance might be in the air. Soon after Christmas, Philip's cousin, King George II of Greece, asked George VI and Queen Elizabeth if they might consider Philip as a suitor for their daughter. To begin with, Princess Elizabeth's parents felt their daughter was too young and inexperienced to be thinking of marriage and they said that Philip should not think any more about it just yet.

Philip spent the rest of the Second World War as first lieutenant on board the new W-class destroyer *Whelp*. He was in the Indian Ocean in December 1944 when a signal arrived from his uncle Dickie Mountbatten (who by now was Supreme Allied Commander Southeast Asia Command) to say that his father, Andrea, had died. This was another blow for Philip, who was unable to attend the funeral of the man he had venerated from a distance but who had played so small a part in his life.

Meanwhile, he and Elizabeth were exchanging letters and each displayed photographs of the other, he in his cabin and she on her bedroom mantelpiece.

Philip enjoyed his war; he did not return to Portsmouth until January 1946 when the *Whelp* arrived home with prisoners of war. He was given the job of overseeing the decommissioning of *Whelp* and then given shore postings, first to a naval training establishment in Wales, before being sent to HMS *Royal Arthur* near Bath, where his job was to teach petty officers. In a letter to Princess Elizabeth he admitted he was 'still not accustomed to the idea of peace, rather fed up with everything ...'

But London was not far away and staff at Buckingham Palace grew accustomed to his little sports car roaring into the forecourt as he rushed inside to see the Princess.

Below: A royal front cover for *The Sketch*, featuring the Princesses Elizabeth and Margaret taking part in the annual pantomime at Windsor Castle in 1942.

OUR PRINCESSES IN PANTO.

Left: Queen Elizabeth with her daughters, Elizabeth and Margaret, photographed by Cecil Beaton at Buckingham Palace in February 1943.

Below: Princess Elizabeth and Prince Philip enjoy each other's company at a wedding reception in December 1946; by this time he had asked for her hand in marriage.

He dined informally with Elizabeth and her sister in the old nursery at the Palace, the three of them clearly enjoying each other's company.

By now Elizabeth was often pestered by people shouting, 'Where's Philip?' as she carried out her engagements and the pair of them tried not to be seen together in public to calm the rising speculation about their future together. In the summer of 1946, he was invited to Balmoral for three weeks to join the royal family as they enjoyed their customary grouse shooting and deer stalking. It is thought this was when he proposed to Princess Elizabeth, who accepted before they went to her parents with the news. The King agreed in principle to the marriage but asked them to wait for a year before making a final decision after Elizabeth's 21st birthday in April 1947. Those close to the King thought he dreaded what he perceived as the loss of his beloved daughter, whose company he always sought when walking and riding out.

Nothing of this was made public, but press speculation mounted dramatically in December 1946 when it became common knowledge that Prince Philip of Greece had applied to become a British citizen.

PERMISSION TO MARRY

Two things happened in the early months of 1947. In February, the royal family – King George and Queen Elizabeth and their daughters the Princesses Elizabeth and Margaret – left a freezing Britain to tour South Africa, Elizabeth's first journey outside the British Isles. On 18 March, *The London Gazette* published details of Philip of Greece's naturalisation as a British citizen. In taking British nationality, he had renounced his royal title, becoming simply Lieutenant Philip Mountbatten RN.

That three-month tour was a testing time for the young couple. The King and Queen thought it a good idea to see if Elizabeth and Philip still felt the same way about each other after their time apart. Philip did not travel to Portsmouth to see them depart on the icy seas on board HMS *Vanguard*, nor was he there to welcome them home in early May, but soon after their return he wrote to the Queen to say that, although he understood the delay had been a good thing, he and Elizabeth would like to start their new life together.

Below: Princess Elizabeth celebrates her twenty-first birthday, 21 April 1947, during her family's state visit to South Africa.

Elizabeth must have had mixed feelings about the tour; she was leaving the man she loved, but she was also experiencing her first taste of the British Commonwealth as it really was. She saw the political tensions in South Africa and she understood that a modern monarchy must nurture the Commonwealth if it was to have a future. She also knew that one day she would be at the head of that monarchy. On her 21st birthday she made an emotional and heartfelt broadcast that was an accurate prediction of the shape her life was to take. The pledges Princess Elizabeth gave from the gardens of Government House, Cape Town, on 21 April 1947, were ones that she has fulfilled through her long reign on the British throne. 'I declare before you that my whole life, whether it be long or short, shall be devoted to your service and the service of our great Imperial family to which we all belong ...,' she vowed. Those listening knew that she meant it.

Once back home, the little sports car was again seen regularly outside the side entrance to Buckingham Palace and, on 7 July, the Queen wrote to her sister, Lady May Elphinstone, that Elizabeth had made up her mind to become engaged to Philip Mountbatten. The Queen added that she thought her daughter was

Left: Crowds gather outside Buckingham Palace, eager to hear news of a royal engagement.

Below: Philip and Elizabeth smile happily at each other as their engagement is announced on 10 July 1947.

really fond of Philip and she prayed they would be very happy. She made it clear that she was telling this news 'very secretly', underlining the words in black and red ink. But the secret had to be kept for two days only. On the evening of 9 July, a Court Circular, issued from Buckingham Palace, read: 'It is with the greatest pleasure that the King and Queen announce the betrothal of their dearly beloved daughter The Princess Elizabeth to Lieutenant Philip Mountbatten, RN, son of the late Prince Andrew of Greece and Princess Andrew (Princess Alice of Battenberg), to which union the King has gladly given his consent.'

Elizabeth wore a platinum engagement ring which sparkled with diamonds that had once belonged to Philip's mother, Alice, who had taken them to a jeweller in Bond Street for it to be made into a new ring.

The following day, spells of bright sunshine broke through the drizzle as the young couple, she flushed and radiant, he uncharacteristically shy, shook hands with guests at a Buckingham Palace garden party. Diplomat and writer Sir Harold Nicolson, who watched the couple, observed that everyone was 'irreverently and shamelessly straining to see the bridal pair'.

A ROYAL WEDDING

Suddenly Philip's life changed. He gained a secretary, a detective to follow him around at a discreet distance and a valet to keep his meagre wardrobe up to scratch and to polish his shoes. He was still living during the week at HMS *Royal Arthur*, at Corsham near Bath, where he taught petty officers the finer points of sea warfare, current affairs and morale. At weekends he would jump into the dark-green leather driving seat of his black MG sports car to make the journey to his grandmother Victoria's apartment at Kensington Palace. His mother, Alice, lived there too at this stage and Philip's close friend David Milford Haven, who was to be his best man, moved in as well to share Philip's spartan attic rooms in the Palace.

Nothing was left to chance. The wedding was scheduled for 20 November 1947 at Westminster Abbey and, six weeks before, Philip was received into the Church of England in a private service, conducted by the Archbishop of Canterbury at Lambeth Palace. Although he had decided not to take a title when he became a British subject, he was now made a Royal Highness and created Baron Greenwich, Earl of Merioneth and Duke of Edinburgh, which acknowledged not only his seafaring background but also included Wales and Scotland in the honours. These peerages were given on the eve of the wedding, so did not appear on the service sheets. Both Philip and Elizabeth were given the Order of the Garter in November – she receiving hers a week before him so that, as future monarch, she had precedence.

Right: Two policemen stand guard over the royal wedding cake, which took over five weeks to make.

Far right: Philip, Duke of Edinburgh, accompanied by his groomsman, the Marquess of Milford Haven, arrives at Westminster Abbey for his wedding to Princess Elizabeth on 20 November 1947.

Rationing was still in place; the previous terrible winter had hit the country hard so everyone agreed the wedding should not be showy or ostentatious. But presents poured in from home and abroad, 1,500 of them going on public display at St James's Palace. An exception was Astrakhan, the thoroughbred chestnut filly sent by the Aga Khan, which became Elizabeth's first flat-race winner. Also on display was the nine-foot-high, four-tier wedding cake, an object of fascination to the British public after years of sugar rationing. Most of the ingredients were given as a wedding present by Australian Girl Guides and one of the panels showed a scene from the night-time battle of Cape Matapan in 1941 when Philip had wielded *Valiant*'s searchlights so effectively (*see pages 22–23*).

Philip enjoyed two stag parties – one an impromptu gathering at The Belfry in the West Midlands, organised by friends; the other on the eve of the wedding at The Dorchester in London, where his uncle, Dickie Mountbatten, was senior guest. The press were invited to this one and Philip left for Kensington Palace just after midnight, reportedly one of the few partygoers who was quite steady on his feet.

On the day of the wedding, his valet, John Dean, brought him his usual 7am tea tray and later reported that the bridegroom was in good form and extremely cheerful. But later, after a breakfast of toast and coffee, Philip confessed to his cousin, Patricia Mountbatten, that he was nervous. Although it was clear to everyone who knew them that he and Elizabeth were in love, theirs was not going to be an ordinary family life. Someday she would be Queen, living in the public spotlight. Philip, an extraordinarily independent man, would have to fall in behind her and give up his freedom.

Elizabeth had asked him to stop smoking, so he and his best man, David Milford Haven, quelled their nerves with a gin and tonic before setting out for Westminster Abbey, Philip

wearing his naval uniform, his new insignia of the Knight Companion Order of the Garter and the ceremonial sword that had belonged to his grandfather, Louis of Battenberg.

Drizzle fell from a grey sky and the wind was bitingly cold. But if Princess Elizabeth had looked out of her Buckingham Palace window early in the morning of her wedding day, she would have seen a sea of people filling the pavements, wrapped in blankets and thick coats, many having slept out overnight to catch a glimpse of the carriage procession.

Despite some newspaper leaders warning against displays of wealth and luxury in post-war Britain, the *Daily Express* had welcomed the forthcoming celebrations, telling the killjoys: 'Life is too drab to pass up this chance of having fun.' Churchill had declared the prospect of a wedding as 'a flash of colour on the hard road we have to travel'.

And colour there was. Here were the Household Brigade back in their rarely seen full-dress uniform: black bearskins with burnished chin-straps, blue trousers adorned with a red stripe and smart blue tunics. The Household Cavalry clattered past, the horses gleaming to challenge the polish on the boots of the

Royal Horse Guards with their blue tunics and red-plumed helmets, and the Life Guards, breastplates sparkling and swords drawn.

Carriages rolled past slowly: the Queen and Princess Margaret, the chief bridesmaid, sitting together in one coach and Queen Mary, holding herself still and ramrod straight, in another. At last came the Glass Coach, drawn by a pair of Windsor Greys and attended by coachmen in scarlet and gold livery. Inside sat Princess Elizabeth, the bride, beautiful in her richly embroidered dress, a double string of pearls, her wedding present from her parents, at her throat and a small tiara, passed down through her family, holding her veil in place. At her side, her father, the King, in the gold-braided and red-sashed blue uniform of Admiral of the Fleet, experienced both intense pride and sadness at his daughter's beauty and his own perceived loss. The crowds cheered as the bride and her father passed by on their way to Westminster Abbey.

Inside was the largest gathering of foreign royalty the country had seen for decades. Among the 2,500 guests were six kings and seven queens, the women wearing full-length ball gowns and the men immaculate in morning dress or dress uniform. Jewellery, taken out of safes and bank vaults for the occasion, sparkled as tiaras, brooches, necklaces and diamonds glittered in the Abbey lights.

There, by the steps of the sacrarium, waiting for his bride, was Prince Philip, his best man by his side. The groom had few relatives in the Abbey to support him. His mother, Alice, sat on the north side, opposite the King and Queen, with her own mother, Victoria, her brother, Dickie, and sister, Louise. From his father's side there was only his uncle, 'Big George', with whom the family had lived in Paris while in exile.

Both the bride and bridegroom made their vows clearly and with conviction. The register was signed before the great Abbey organ swelled with sound and the bells rang out as the Duke and Duchess of Edinburgh, now man and wife, walked slowly, arm in arm, down the length of the ancient church.

Back at Buckingham Palace, the couple had to appear on the balcony three times to satisfy the thousands waiting below. After a wedding breakfast for 150 in the gold-and-white Supper Room, they changed and left the Palace in a shower of rose petals to drive through the November frosts in an open landau to Waterloo Station. From here, they travelled by train to honeymoon at Broadlands, the home of the Mountbattens. Tucked under their rugs were a couple of hot-water bottles and Susan, Princess Elizabeth's favourite pet corgi.

Below: Philip and Elizabeth, man and wife, leave the Abbey.

Opposite top: Queen Elizabeth and Princess Margaret arrive at Westminster Abbey for the wedding.

Opposite: Princess Elizabeth, accompanied by her father, King George VI, arrives at the altar for her wedding in Westminster Abbey. Her train is held by the Princes William of Gloucester and Michael of Kent.

A royal wedding: the Duke of Edinburgh and Princess Elizabeth, with his best man and her bridesmaids and page boys at Buckingham Palace.

MARRIED LIFE

Philip and Elizabeth spent the first few days of married life in Hampshire at the Mountbattens' beautiful Palladian mansion, Broadlands, by the River Test. But it was not a peaceful stay. The telephone rang incessantly and whenever the newly-weds stepped outside for a walk or a ride in the grounds, they and their bodyguards were aware that reporters and curious members of the public had somehow managed to climb trees or scramble onto the top of the wall in their eagerness to catch a glimpse of the royal couple. Their Sunday visit to Romsey Abbey for matins saw inquisitive people climbing over tombstones, while some even propped ladders against the church windows to peer in at the glamorous pair. But this did not seem to worry them. Elizabeth wrote to her mother after a couple of days that Philip was 'an angel', kind and thoughtful, and that living with him and having him around all the time was 'just perfect'.

After a week at Broadlands, Philip and Elizabeth travelled to Scotland to stay at Birkhall, a royal hunting lodge on the Balmoral estate, where at last they could enjoy some privacy. The snow lay thickly upon the ground, but they and the corgis were cosy in front of roaring log fires.

All too soon it was time to return to London and a home of their own – which turned out to be something of a problem. They were to have lived in Sunninghill Park near Windsor, but the country house had mysteriously burnt down, while Clarence House, their designated London residence, was still in need of renovation, having been damaged by bombs and neglect during the war. For three months they were lent Clock House at Kensington Palace, but when the owners, the Earl and Countess of Athlone, returned from abroad, the young couple had to move into Elizabeth's former

Below:
The newly-weds: Philip and Elizabeth on honeymoon at Broadlands in Hampshire.

Below right:
Windlesham Moor, the couple's first home after their marriage.

Clarence House, which was to become the newly-weds' London residence, had been the home of the Duke of Connaught, son of Queen Victoria. It was already dilapidated on his death in 1942. Today it is a working residence, the London home of Prince Charles, the Duchess of Cornwall and Prince Harry; the mansion, which lies next to St James's Palace, cost £78,000 to restore for Elizabeth and Philip (around £2.3 million in current terms). Furnishing it was easy — there were more than enough wedding presents to ensure a comfortable home.

Left: The Duke of Connaught in 1947: Queen Victoria's son was the last occupant of Clarence House before it was renovated for Philip and Elizabeth.

Below: Like all newly married couples, Philip and Elizabeth set up home with their wedding gifts – and were clearly delighted when they received this electric sewing machine from the people of Clydebank.

apartments in Buckingham Palace. Philip, longing for a home of his own, found this far from ideal with a lack of privacy and endless protocol to endure.

By this time, Philip had a desk job as an operations officer at the Admiralty, just a short walk down the Mall from the Palace, but he later admitted that, used as he had been to active service at sea, the work was often frustrating.

However, they were soon renting Windlesham Moor, a country house in Berkshire, for weekend use and Philip threw himself into home-making with enthusiasm; he enjoyed having a settled place of his own for the first time since early childhood. The house, set in 50 acres (20ha) near Sunningdale, was not grand by royal standards, but had a large drawing room, five main bedrooms, a dining room, hall and study, a 'Chinese' room, games room and staff quarters.

During the week Philip became used to his working life being interrupted by engagements that he and his new wife carried out both separately and together, and by 'lessons' that the pair undertook on the political and diplomatic situations around the world. Soon the time came when they were to make their first official trip abroad – a four-day visit to Paris to cement diplomatic ties with France, the country that had been their wartime ally.

A TRIP
TO PARIS

By the time the new year, 1948, was rung in, Philip knew that there was no long-term hope for a career in the Navy, although later that year he moved from the Admiralty to a staff course at the Royal Naval College, Greenwich, spending the greater part of the week at the college and coming home at weekends.

At that time, and for the first four years of his marriage, Philip managed to combine his day job with the Navy with his royal duties, slipping back to change out of uniform to attend charity functions, church services, business meetings and factory tours. It soon became apparent that his natural charm was an asset at these events. His detractors (and there were some among the courtiers at the Palace) had to concede that he carried out the duties that were going to be his for life in an exemplary fashion. Observers noticed that he was a good speaker, rarely, if ever, using notes and never stumbling over his words or at a loss for a phrase. He was witty and smiled in a relaxed way as he spoke. An *Evening Standard* columnist was certainly captivated, writing: 'The more I hear Prince Philip speak in public, the more impressed I am by his ability,' going on to remark that royalty had not produced a speaker of such charm and friendliness since the days of the Prince of Wales.

Right: Elizabeth and Philip outside the British Embassy during their visit to Paris in May 1948; they had yet to announce that Princess Elizabeth was expecting their first child.

In February that year, there was a chance for Philip to try out his undoubted charm on a larger audience – the people of France. The Edinburghs were told by Elizabeth's private secretary, Sir John 'Jock' Colville, of the four-day official visit to Paris that had been arranged for May. It was to be their first trip abroad together and, on the face of it, the visit was a huge success. Elizabeth, a beautiful and fashionable princess, heir presumptive to the British throne, and her handsome young husband were a dream couple. They delighted the French people who, overnight, fell in love with the charming English royals. They were taken to the best Paris had to offer – Versailles, the opera and on a riverboat down the Seine. They attended lunches and dinners, a banquet and receptions, and both spoke French well – Philip through his childhood years in Paris and Elizabeth thanks to a good tutor.

But what their hosts did not realise was that both were feeling unwell during the tour. The weather was sweltering – the hottest weekend in Paris for decades – and the four-day schedule was impossibly crowded. Philip had fallen victim to mild food poisoning, although he carried out his duties diligently while having to take breaks along the way. Elizabeth, always polite and charming, seemed tired and at one point she had to leave a reception thrown by the British Embassy in her honour, meeting only half the guests lining up to shake her hand. Philip was less than happy when, dining with a small party at a restaurant, he spotted a badly hidden camera lens pointing straight at their table. But as a public relations exercise and a diplomatic mission, the visit was deemed to be a triumph.

Word of Elizabeth's bouts of tiredness and listlessness spread and it was soon rumoured that she might be expecting a baby. But nothing was certain until an announcement came from the Palace in early June to the effect that the Princess would undertake no public engagements from the end of the month. It was not hard to crack the carefully worded Buckingham Palace code: Elizabeth and Philip were expecting their first child.

FATHERHOOD

King George VI's private secretary, Sir Alan 'Tommy' Lascelles, rushed across to the Buckingham Palace squash court where Prince Philip and his friend and equerry Mike Parker were having an energetic game. It was the second squash session in an evening that had also seen Philip take a swim in the Palace pool. Although he played as competitively as usual, his mind was elsewhere. It was the evening of 14 November 1948, almost one year after his wedding.

As soon as Tommy Lascelles delivered his message, Philip raced back upstairs, stopping only to scoop up the roses, carnations and bottle of champagne he had ready. He entered the Palace's Buhl Room, now converted into a clinical delivery suite, to see his wife, semi-conscious from the medication, and his newborn baby son lying safely in a cot. Philip opened the champagne for the medical and household staff to toast the health of the tiny child and, by the time Elizabeth opened her eyes, he was by her side with his bouquet to kiss her and take her hand.

Elizabeth had gone into labour more than 24 hours earlier and Philip, never the most patient of men, had waited restlessly for the birth. Friends saw that he was thrilled to have a son and, that evening, he sent a telegram to his mother, Princess Alice, now living in Greece, to tell her the happy news.

'Her Royal Highness the Princess Elizabeth, Duchess of Edinburgh, was safely delivered of a Prince at 9.14 o'clock this evening. Her Royal Highness and the infant prince are both doing well,' read the handwritten notice attached to the Palace railings by the King's press secretary that evening. Even though it was getting on for midnight, there was already a crowd of more than 3,000 waiting to hear the news. When the notice had been read there was sustained cheering and an impromptu rendition of 'For he's a jolly good fellow!'

Within 24 hours, more than 4,000 telegrams had been received and the presents, from hand-knitted bootees and matinee jackets to teddy bears, began to

Left: Her husband at her shoulder, Princess Elizabeth holds her son, Prince Charles, after his christening.

Left: Prince Philip holds his baby son, while Princess Elizabeth looks on.

Below: Princess Alice of Greece, Prince Philip's mother, photographed in 1953. She is seen here arriving in London to attend the coronation of her daughter-in-law.

pour in. But what everyone wanted to know was the baby's name, which was not announced until his christening, a full month later.

When the country learnt, on 15 December, that the baby Prince was to be called Charles, there was some surprise as the name had not been used by the royal family for more than 300 years, after the unhappy reigns of the two monarchs of that same name. However, both parents liked the name and Charles Philip Arthur George was christened in the presence of eight godparents (or 'sponsors' in royal circles), three of them Philip's relations – his grandmother Victoria Milford Haven, his uncle 'Big' Prince George of Greece and his cousin Patricia Brabourne. Another godparent, King Haakon of Norway, was related to both Philip and Elizabeth.

Parenthood suited the young couple,

Philip's mother, Princess Alice, now fully recovered from her illness, was delighted at the birth of a new grandson. She was living on the Greek island of Tinos where she dressed in a nun-like habit and planned to train young women to become nursing sisters. She wrote to Philip as soon as she received the telegram, 'I think of you so much with a sweet baby of your own, of your joy and the interest you will take in all his little doings.'

who at that time were relatively free to spend time with their baby son. Prince Philip was known to be a good and involved father with all his children when they were little – playing with them, reading stories and teaching them to fish and enjoy outdoor pursuits.

A HAPPY TIME

At last, in July 1949, Clarence House was ready for occupation. The Edinburghs, with their eight-month-old son, were more than happy to move. Philip was especially excited at the prospect of his first real home since he was a nine-year-old boy living at St Cloud, Paris. He and Elizabeth had visited the house daily in the 18 months it had taken to repair the damage and redecorate – even, in Elizabeth's case, helping to mix the dining-room paint to ensure the correct shade of green. They had talked to their staff to ensure that 'below stairs' was ideal too, so that everyone was happy. There were radios in each staff bedroom and desks furnished with writing paper and blotting pads. Wedding presents taken out of storage included enough armchairs and other items to furnish the staff bedrooms as well as the rest of the house.

In the basement was a cinema given as a wedding present by a society representing film companies. Philip's bedroom, panelled with Scottish sycamore and with an oatmeal carpet, contained many electronic gadgets designed to make life simpler. Hanging in his bathrooms were pictures of the ships on which he had served during the war. Thoroughly enjoying having a home of his own at last, Philip would make a tour of the whole house when he arrived back after time away, having a chat with everyone – just like a naval officer returning to his ship after shore leave.

Despite the luxury of Clarence House and the enjoyment of family life, Philip still yearned for some time at sea and, in the autumn of 1949, with the permission of his father-in-law, King George VI, he returned to active service, flying out to Malta as second-in-command of *Chequers*, the ship that led the first destroyer flotilla of the Mediterranean Fleet. While he waited for *Chequers* to undergo a refit, he stayed with the Mountbattens at their luxurious Villa Guardamangia, perched high in the hills at Pieta.

Elizabeth flew out to Malta in November to join Philip and celebrate their second wedding anniversary. Young Charles was left at home with his nursery staff and fond grandparents. If the Mountbattens were apprehensive about having the future Queen of England to stay, they were soon won over by her charm and kindness.

Below: The Duke of Edinburgh at his desk in Buckingham Palace in August 1951.

'Lilibet is quite enchanting and I've lost whatever of my heart is left to spare entirely to her,' Dickie Mountbatten wrote to his daughter, Patricia, just before Christmas. 'She dances quite divinely and always wants a samba when we dance together,' he added.

Elizabeth found life on Malta extraordinarily liberating. Although everyone on the island knew who she was, no one would have dreamt of intruding on her privacy. No sightseers hung around outside the villa and she was free to come and go as she pleased. For the first time in her life she was able to lead a comparatively ordinary existence, driving her own Daimler, taking herself to the hairdresser and on shopping expeditions and joining in happily with the other Navy wives with their coffee mornings and drinks parties.

When Philip was on shore, they would eat out and dance together at hotels and restaurants and enjoy boating trips to local beaches and creeks, swimming, sunbathing and eating picnics – just like everybody else. 'It's lovely seeing her so radiant and leading a more or less human existence for once,' Edwina Mountbatten wrote to her friend, Indian Prime Minister Jawaharlal Nehru. Elizabeth stayed with her husband and the Mountbattens until the end of December, enjoying Christmas with them, until *Chequers* was detailed to patrol the Red Sea with six other warships.

Above: Prince Philip with his five-month-old son, Prince Charles.

Below: Prince Philip and Princess Elizabeth on a balcony overlooking the sea at the Villa Guardamangia in Malta, 1949.

CAREFREE DAYS

Elizabeth, by now expecting their second baby, joined Philip for another six weeks in the spring of 1950. In June that year, Philip was made lieutenant commander and given his first command, the frigate *Magpie*, but before he was piped aboard in September, he returned home on leave to await the birth of the next child. He was reunited with his mother, Alice, who, wanting to see her two British grandchildren, had travelled over from Tinos.

Back in Malta, Philip was determined to make *Magpie* the best ship in the fleet – and to win the annual regatta. The crew might not have been so happy as he made them practise until their hands blistered, but they applauded 'Dukey', as they called him, when *Magpie*'s masthead was adorned with a large red cockerel for coming first in six out of the 10 competitions.

Because of his new command, he was unable to attend the funeral of his grandmother, Victoria Milford Haven, in late September, and this must have been a cause for regret as she, as much as anyone, had looked after him through his childhood.

He did return, briefly, for the christening of his baby daughter, Anne, in October and was reunited with Elizabeth in late November when she flew out to Malta, leaving the children in the good care of nannies and grandparents. Again they lived at Villa Guardamangia and it was during this time that Philip began to play polo at which he soon excelled. In December, he and Elizabeth sailed for Greece – the Princess's first visit to her husband's homeland, where they stayed with the royal family and were welcomed warmly by the Greek people.

Right: Philip as Commander of the frigate HMS *Magpie* in 1951.

Far right: The royal family at Balmoral in 1951 with the newest addition to the family, Princess Anne.

Philip knew that his naval career would end one day soon. Worries were increasing over his father-in-law's failing health and plans were already in place for the Edinburghs to make an official tour of Canada in autumn 1951. In July 1951, they left Malta for the last time, Philip on 'indefinite leave' from the Navy, a matter of some remorse. But he knew that he would have to support Elizabeth who was beginning to take on many of her parents' public duties and whose workload was now considerable.

During the summer, she read the King's speech at a state banquet for King Haakon of Norway and, for the first time, took the salute at Trooping the Colour, sitting ramrod straight and mounted side-saddle on a well-trained police horse. In September that year, the King underwent an operation to remove his left lung in a bid to contain the cancer which, unbeknown to him, had just been diagnosed. Philip, for so long the leader and instigator, saw his future clearly – he would always have to play a supporting role to his wife in her duties as heir to the throne and, eventually, Queen. But there was no reason why he should not take on some duties of his own.

He started with his inaugural address to the British Association for the Advancement of Science, an organisation of which he had become president. He wrote his own address which he had planned in his cabin aboard *Magpie*, cluttering the confined space with books and papers for the talk, entitled 'The British Contribution to Science and Technology in the Past Hundred Years'. Philip referred to the Great Exhibition of 1851, a huge science fair masterminded by his great-great-grandfather, Prince Albert, that took place in the Crystal Palace in Hyde Park. The address was received with enthusiasm by the press and members of the scientific community, and *The Times* later gave thanks that 'The Queen should be supported by a personality of outstanding vitality who is in step with the march of the modern world'.

CONQUERING CANADA

It was typical of Philip that, as he and Princess Elizabeth took off for their postponed Canadian trip on 7 October 1951, just two weeks after the King's operation, he asked to join the pilots on the flight deck of the BOAC stratocruiser to learn about the controls.

There had been debate about the flight – no member of the royal family had crossed the Atlantic by air before and Winston Churchill, then leader of the opposition, was vocal in his opposition to Elizabeth taking the risk. But Philip, despite the air accident which had claimed the lives of his sister and her family, prevailed and they arrived at Montreal to a 21-gun salute and a warm welcome from Canadian Prime Minister Louis St Laurent and Governor General Field Marshall Viscount Alexander of Tunis.

Elizabeth's anxiety about the state of her father's health often showed but the Canadians put her sometimes sombre expression down to shyness. Philip smiled and chatted. He unbent and was willing to try anything, from handling the controls of the royal train to taking the wheel of the barge along the Ottawa River and occupying the co-pilot's seat of the Royal Canadian Air Force plane which they used frequently to cover the 10,000 miles (16,000km) of all seven Canadian provinces.

He was solicitous over Elizabeth, supporting her in this, their first major overseas trip together. If Philip was the star turn in Canada, Princess Elizabeth captivated American hearts on their brief stopover in Washington, before returning home in the liner *Empress of Scotland*. President Truman declared: 'When I was a little boy I read about a fairy princess, and here she is!' *The Washington Post* concurred, writing that the Princess had '... charmed and captivated this city ...'.

When they arrived home, the King, delighted by their success, made both Elizabeth and Philip Privy Counsellors. Churchill, now prime minister once more after the general election towards the end of October, told them the whole nation was grateful for what they had done.

The couple's next tour was to be a big one – East Africa, Australia and New Zealand. They were to travel as representatives of the King and, in preparation, Philip spent his spare time studying Australian affairs in general and learning about sheep farming in particular. But first came Christmas at Sandringham where the King, now not at all well, was in a happy mood because he had already recorded his 'live' Christmas Day message, something that he normally dreaded for weeks beforehand. But he enjoyed Christmas,

Below:
Wrapped up warmly, the Duke of Edinburgh and Princess Elizabeth enjoy the drama of the Calgary stampede during their tour of Canada in autumn 1951.

managing to go out shooting and to the theatre where the royal family applauded a performance of *South Pacific* at the Theatre Royal, Drury Lane. The following day King George, Queen Elizabeth and Winston Churchill were at London Airport to see Elizabeth and Philip off to Kenya, their first stop on the Antipodean tour.

Two days of engagements were followed by time off at Sagana Lodge in the Aberdare mountains. The pair fished and rode and sunned themselves before travelling to Treetops, a 'tree house' built in the branches of a giant fig, where animals may be observed at the water holes beneath. Midnight came and they spent the early hours of 6 February filming and recording elephants, rhinoceros and baboons. While the couple were in Africa marvelling at the wildlife, back home Elizabeth's father was found dead in his bed by his manservant bringing in the early morning tea.

Communication was slow in 1952. Elizabeth and Philip were back at Sagana Lodge, she writing letters, he having a nap, when the sad news was brought by Philip's equerry, Mike Parker. Philip, shocked, went to Elizabeth and, asking her to walk in the garden, told her gently that her father had died.

The tour was over and real life was about to begin for the new queen and her consort.

Above: Members of the royal family, including King George VI, Queen Elizabeth and Princess Margaret, wave farewell as Elizabeth and Philip's aeroplane, taking them on their tour of Kenya in early 1952, rolls down the runway. Elizabeth was not to see her father again. The King died on 6 February.

Left: The royal couple in the grounds of Royal Lodge, Sagana, their wedding present from the people of Kenya.

BECOMING CONSORT

It was mid-afternoon on a freezing cold February day and a BOAC Argonaut aircraft touched down at London Airport. Waiting on the tarmac were four grave, dark-coated figures. A slight woman, dressed in black, walked alone down the aircraft steps. Queen Elizabeth II was greeted by her prime minister, a tearful Winston Churchill, who had first become a member of parliament when her great-great-grandmother, Queen Victoria, was on the throne. With him were Clement Attlee, Anthony Eden and Frederick Marquis, the Earl of Woolton.

Philip, conscious that from now on his place was behind his wife, waited until she was stepping to the ground before he walked slowly from the cabin.

The following day, he escorted his wife from Clarence House through the snow to St James's Palace where her privy councillors were waiting to hear her read out her declaration of sovereignty in a thin, high voice. There were tears in many eyes as she closed by saying: 'My heart is too full for me to say more to you today than that I shall always work as my father did throughout his reign ... I pray that God will help me to discharge worthily this heavy task that has been laid on me so early in my life.' Philip stepped forward and led her quietly to the car. Elizabeth was tearful; she mourned her father and contemplated the enormous task ahead. Philip knew that their carefree days were over. He understood that family days in his beloved home, Clarence House, were behind him and that they would have to move to Buckingham Palace. He also knew that there was no chance of further service in the Royal Navy.

Below: Prince Philip and his wife, now Queen Elizabeth II, are met at London Airport as they return following the death of King George VI.

Although he was powerless to prevent the move, he decided to modernise the way things were done at the palace. He set up an Organisation and Methods Review, asking every single member of staff what they were doing and why, and visited each of the 600 rooms to see what went on. Some of the older courtiers were horrified, but on the whole Philip's questions and changes went down well.

He now had his own office (which included five secretaries, pages, valets, a chauffeur, a chief clerk and a police officer) run by his treasurer, Sir Frederick 'Boy' Browning, husband of novelist Daphne du Maurier. Philip was already patron of a large number of organisations – mostly to do with sport, science, education or the sea – and held honorary appointments in the armed forces, including that of Admiral of the Fleet.

Not content with his prowess at sea, he decided he should learn to fly. This was 1952 and palace officials tried to dissuade him because of the perceived dangers, but Philip was not to be deterred. He put forward spurious reasons, such as saving time when undertaking one-day engagements but, in truth, for him it was the indignity of wearing new RAF Marshal uniform without having earned the wings that went with it. His first lesson was in November 1952. By late December he had completed his first solo flight, in a Chipmunk, going on to receive his wings in early May 1953, just a month before the coronation.

As with everything that required skilful hand-to-eye coordination and judgement, he excelled and became an outstanding pilot, often taking the controls to fly the royal family to Scotland for their summer holidays and flying his eldest son, Prince Charles, to Gordonstoun at the start of a new term.

Above: Philip, who learnt to fly in the early 1950s, at the controls of a Heron of the Queen's flight in 1958.

THE CORONATION

Excitement mounted and sales of television and wireless sets soared as the coronation day drew near. Tuesday 2 June 1953 was the chosen date, asserted by the weather forecasters to be the most reliably sunny day of the year.

In the event, however, it rained. More than half a million people had camped on the pavements running alongside the route from Buckingham Palace to Westminster Abbey, but no one seemed to mind the drizzle as they excitedly watched the carriages and cars of guests drive slowly past.

Official rehearsals for the ceremony had taken place in Westminster Abbey. Unofficially, at home, Philip and Elizabeth had rehearsed in Buckingham Palace ballroom, he tying bed sheets together to mimic her long coronation train.

On the day itself, Philip's family was well represented. His mother, Alice, wore a new, specially made grey robe and she progressed to her seat in the royal box with her son's three sisters – Margarita, Theodora and Sophie – and their husbands. In front of them were the Queen Mother, Princess Margaret and four-year-old Prince Charles dressed in a white satin suit. Queen Mary, sadly, did not live to see her granddaughter crowned; she died on 24 March, 10 weeks earlier, leaving instructions that mourning for her death was not to interfere with the ceremony.

Philip and Elizabeth, travelling in the Gold State Coach drawn by eight Windsor Greys, were accompanied by postilions and footmen, the Yeomen of the Guard, the Sovereign's Escort, the Queen's Bargemaster and a dozen Watermen. Mounted officers flanking the coach included the Master of the Horse, the Lord High Constable, Gold-Stick-in-Waiting, Silver-Stick-in-Waiting, personal aides-de-camp and equerries. The whole procession was magnificent and the crowd, having been starved of colour and ceremony through the war and the austerity years that followed, roared their approval.

Queen Elizabeth walked down the aisle without Philip by her side; he, resplendent in his uniform of Admiral of the Fleet, decorated with gold epaulettes and the Garter Star, was part of the preceding procession. But he was the first to pay homage to her after the crowning: 'I, Philip, Duke of Edinburgh, do become your liege man of life and limb and of earthly worship,' he vowed as he knelt

Below:
Prince Charles and Princess Anne, looked after by their grandmother, salute their mother on her Coronation Day.

before her and placed his hands between hers. As he rose to his feet he touched her crown and kissed her tenderly on the cheek.

Afterwards they posed for photographs taken by Cecil Beaton, who confessed later that the smile on Philip's lips put 'the fear of God' into him. Beaton, who said that he admired Philip enormously and thought he was first-rate at putting people at ease and making small talk, was nevertheless somewhat nervous of his 'rather ragging' attitude towards formal proceedings.

The Queen settled into her new role. She had seen her father carrying out his duties, and she knew what she had to do: reading the contents of her 'boxes' each day, giving audiences, signing papers, conducting investitures, dealing with affairs of state thoroughly and conscientiously.

Prince Philip, who had largely needed to make his own way in life, had no figure on which to model himself. He had to find a way to support his wife while using his considerable talent and energy. He became the Queen's eyes and ears, travelling around the country, visiting factories and offices, hospitals and mines, keeping her informed of the feeling in the country. He became involved with hundreds of organisations, all of which valued his enthusiasm as a patron. In 1956, he not only set up the Commonwealth Study Conferences but also, with the help of his old headmaster, Kurt Hahn, founded the Duke of Edinburgh Award – one of his greatest achievements because of the impact the scheme has had on the lives of millions of young people.

Above left: Philip pays homage to his wife, the newly crowned Queen, as she sits on her coronation throne in Westminster Abbey.

Above: Crowds gather in the streets of London on Coronation Day.

A LIFE OF DUTY

Philip, not involved with the daily intricacies of affairs of state, took charge when it came to running the royal estates, deciding on the children's education, setting up his charities and being on parade with the Queen when state events beckoned and official visits required their presence.

He has always been at her side at the State Opening of Parliament, standing, head bowed, before the Cenotaph on Remembrance Sunday, at the Royal Maundy Presentation, the Garter Ceremony and at Trooping the Colour on her official birthday, in June. The Season, which revolves around open-air celebrations such as the Queen's Garden Parties at Buckingham Palace and at Holyrood Palace in Edinburgh, the Chelsea Flower Show, Royal Ascot and Derby Day, have always seen the royal couple together, enjoying the company and the event – especially those in the racing calendar.

Below: Prince Philip and the Queen share a joke as they arrive at Westminster for the State Opening of Parliament in May 2013.

Philip has stood side by side with Her Majesty when visiting royalty or when heads of state were being entertained at Buckingham Palace and has been there, a step or two behind, whenever she makes her own visits, endlessly shaking hands, making small talk and expressing interest in the doings of groups and organisations at home and abroad.

The Queen has rarely travelled abroad without the Duke of Edinburgh, but he has made many solo visits on behalf of Great Britain, the Commonwealth and the causes he supported. The longest of these tours away from his family was in 1956 when he set off in October in HMS *Britannia*, commissioned just two years earlier and later used by the royal family for more than 43 years. The tour was to last four months, its primary purpose to open the Olympic Games in Melbourne, Australia, in November that year. It was the first time the Games had been held south of the equator and *Britannia* was chosen as the mode of transport so that the Duke could visit as many of the more remote British dependencies – most accessible only by sea – as possible. The tour took him to New Zealand, Ceylon, the Gambia, Antarctica (where he became the first member of the royal family to cross into the Antarctic Circle) and the Falkland Islands. Many of the smaller islands had never before been visited by a member of the royal family.

THE DUKE OF EDINBURGH'S AWARD

The year 1956 was full of activity for the Duke, who founded his much-praised award which encouraged young people to embark on outdoor adventure and achieve self-reliance, physical fitness, endeavour, enterprise and compassion; the qualities that his old headmaster instilled into the boys at Gordonstoun. The first Duke of Edinburgh's Award adventure took place in February 1957 when a group of boys, rucksacks on their backs, gathered together for that inaugural expedition. Nowadays, both girls and boys take part in activities such as volunteering, physical fitness, skills and expeditions. Since that first adventure, more than five million young people in the UK (and eight million worldwide) have participated in The Duke of Edinburgh's Award (DofE), which has given the taste for the outdoor life to people such as David Hempleman-Adams, one of Britain's greatest adventurers. David later admitted that his first DofE Award expedition as a young teenager gave him the thirst for exploration and challenge that led him to undertake his often dangerous and record-breaking Arctic, Antarctic and mountaineering exploits.

Above: The Queen and Prince Philip entertain America's first couple, President John Kennedy and his wife, Jackie, at Buckingham Palace in June 1961.

Above: Philip feeds penguins in the Antarctic in January 1957 during his round-the-world tour aboard the Royal Yacht *Britannia*.

Although there was adverse comment in the press at the time to the effect that he should be at home spending Christmas with his wife and small children, the Queen was quite happy for him to go. She told the world in her Christmas message that year: 'If my husband cannot be at home on Christmas Day, I could not wish for a better reason than he should be travelling in other parts of the Commonwealth.'

MAN OF ACTION

Below: Philip at the helm of the yacht *Bluebottle* during Cowes week in 1957. Prince Charles is on board, as are Philip's yachting advisor, Uffa Fox, and Sailing Master of *Bluebottle*, Lieutenant Commander Alistair Easton.

It was in the early days of his marriage that Philip started playing polo, a game enjoyed by his Uncle Dickie Mountbatten. While Philip was serving in Malta with the Royal Navy, he and his uncle would spend time off water skiing and spear fishing. Mountbatten suggested that his nephew should join him on the polo field. Philip initially rejected the idea, saying he preferred to play hockey with his shipmates. Elizabeth was also keen for him to take up polo but she knew that Philip would not respond well to being badgered into doing anything. She cautioned Mountbatten to let him come round to it in his own time – and he did, becoming an expert player and enjoying the game with a passion while he was a young man.

In 1971, he hung up his polo mallet and took up carriage driving, another sport at which he excelled, going on to represent Britain at several European and World Championships. In 1968, as president of the International Equestrian Foundation, he started the process which resulted in new rules for the modern horse driving trials. Competitions are tough, requiring skill in dressage, precision-driving through cones and a cross-country marathon obstacle course.

Left: Philip playing polo in 1963.

Opposite right: The Duke takes the reins at the Royal Windsor Horse Show in 1994.

He never lost his love of the sea and spent many hours sailing with his friend Uffa Fox on the south coast and with his family on the Royal Yacht *Britannia*. Both he and the Queen were extremely upset when *Britannia*, the starting point for so many happy trips and holidays, was decommissioned in December 1997.

Prince Philip always enjoyed an outdoor life. On his marriage in 1947, his wife was more than happy for him to take on the management of the royal estates, where he became an expert shot and a good fisherman – and a dab hand at cooking the family lunch on the barbecue during the summer holidays.

PHILIP AT HOME

Philip famously complained about the move to the 'museum' and the 'tied cottage' when he and Elizabeth, with their two young children, had to move from Clarence House into Buckingham Palace. His rootless childhood left him with a fierce need for a secure home of his own; Clarence House had satisfied that need. But the move had to be made and the couple ensured that their apartments were, in contrast to the magnificent State Rooms, modern and homely. It was here that their two younger sons, Andrew and Edward, were born in 1960 and 1964 respectively.

Buckingham Palace, Windsor Castle and the Palace of Holyroodhouse in Edinburgh do not belong to the royal family, but to the nation. However, the two 'holiday' estates – Sandringham in Norfolk and Balmoral in Scotland – are the Queen's own properties and it is here that Philip has always been able to relax and enjoy the outdoor pursuits that gave him so much pleasure.

The whole royal family gathers at Sandringham in north Norfolk for Christmas, meeting on Christmas Eve over tea laid out on sideboards in the Saloon, the imposing entrance hall. Then, as is the European custom, presents are exchanged, but the gifts are tokens, the rule being that, for the adults anyway, they must be inexpensive and practical. The children do better, with stockings full of exciting toys.

A black-tie dinner follows, eaten by candlelight at a table laid with shining silverware and beautiful china and decorated with greenery from the estate. Food is fresh and local – seafood caught off the Norfolk coast, beef, lamb or game from the estate and a pudding made with fruit grown on the family farms. Sitting quietly in a corner may be the Queen's corgis who, at her signal, leave the room with the ladies, while the Duke of Edinburgh serves brandy or port to the men.

Below left: Prince Philip and the Queen with their youngest sons, Princes Andrew and Edward, at Balmoral in 1972.

Below right: Windsor Castle, a favourite family home.

Stockings hang at the bottom of every bed on Christmas morning and, once these have been opened and breakfast eaten, the house party walks to St Mary Magdalene church for the Christmas Day service, greeting members of the public on the way. Christmas lunch of estate-bred turkey is followed by a cosy afternoon sitting by the fire and watching the Queen give her now pre-recorded Christmas Message on the television.

Much of the holiday time for the royal family is spent outdoors, riding, walking and shooting, and an outdoor summer holiday is what Prince Philip has enjoyed at Balmoral Castle, the Queen's Scottish home, set in an 11,000-acre (4,450ha) estate. During the two-month summer stay, guests – from old friends and government ministers to visiting heads of state and royalty – have traditionally been invited, but they have to be prepared to join in with the daily programme of outdoor pursuits prepared and organised by Prince Philip.

Above: The Duke opts for a leisurely ride on his mini motorbike round the Sandringham Horse Trials in 2005.

If the family are on their own they might pile picnic baskets, dogs and wet-weather gear into a couple of four-wheel-drive vehicles, one with Her Majesty at the wheel, and make for an isolated corner of Loch Muick where stands a small house built for Queen Victoria, who was great-great-grandmother to both Prince Philip and The Queen. This is their base camp for the day, from where they set off through the heather to walk and fish before coming back to a picnic or food cooked on the barbecue by Prince Philip.

Windsor Castle, just 20 miles (30km) from London but set in the peaceful 5,700 acres (2,300ha) of Windsor Great Park, is where Prince Philip and the Queen have enjoyed spending Easter and many weekends. The Queen has for decades enjoyed relaxing rides, while Prince Philip might, in his younger days, have spent hours practising polo and carriage driving.

Left: Led by the Duke of Edinburgh, the royal family attends a Christmas Day service at Sandringham in 2012. Walking alongside the Duke are his youngest son, Prince Edward, and his wife Sophie, Countess of Wessex, and daughter Lady Louise Windsor.

JOY AND SORROW

Both the Queen and Prince Philip have had their share of joy and sorrow, she losing her father when he was just 56 and taking on the enormous duty as Queen when she was still a young wife and mother. But it was a role she had been preparing for since the age of 10, and her childhood was a happy and secure one.

Right: Philip, aged eight, wearing Greek national costume at his school in St Cloud, Paris, in 1929.

Above: Braving the elements, 3 June 2012: Philip celebrates his wife's diamond jubilee on board the *Spirit of Chartwell* which led the magnificent river pageant in honour of the Queen's 60 years on the throne.

The death of Diana, Princess of Wales in 1997 was one of the saddest times for the royal family. Prince Philip and the Queen saw it particularly as a private tragedy for their two grandsons, Diana and Charles's sons, Prince William and Prince Harry. But, of course, it could not be kept private as a whole nation joined in the mourning. Prince Charles and Diana's younger brother, Charles Spencer, were to walk behind her coffin at the funeral. The two young Princes, William and Harry, were uncertain if they should do the same. It was Prince Philip, perhaps mindful of the time when he, as a young man, had walked in the funeral procession of his sister, Cecile, who told William that he might regret it later if he did not join the cortège. Philip supported the boys by walking with them himself.

Philip, however, had a particularly disrupted childhood. Fortunately, he was too young to understand the sadness and fear felt by his parents and sisters as they fled their villa in Corfu to go into exile in late 1922, but when he was seven, he was old enough to know something was wrong when his mother, Alice, began suffering the delusions that led to her breakdown and eventual committal to a sanatorium. By the time he was nine, he was at boarding school and in the care of his English grandmother and uncles. The break-up of his family happened gradually, but it must have been the cause of anxiety and sorrow for the young boy.

Philip found happiness and security at Gordonstoun in Scotland (*see pages 18–19*) where the spartan but fulfilling regime suited his independent spirit and active nature, and he later enjoyed his course at Dartmouth Royal Naval College, where the promise of a career in the Royal Navy proved to be all that he wanted at that time. Perhaps the biggest tragedy of his young life was the death of his sister Cecile, her husband and sons in a plane crash near Ostend, when Philip was 16 and still at Gordonstoun.

Marriage to Princess Elizabeth brought love, security, a family and a home of his own. Their first few years, before the Queen succeeded her father to the throne, were happy ones for both of them. Philip loved his job and proved to be excellent at it. It was the view of many that if he had been able to pursue his naval career he would have emulated his grandfather and uncle in becoming First Sea Lord on pure merit.

But although he may have had a heavy heart at the burden of sovereignty that was his wife's and his by default, he did not bend under the pressure. His nature was to innovate and excel and this he always did, sharing the milestones of a long and fruitful reign, seeing a quarter of a century, then half a century, of faithful service until, in 2012, he and the Queen celebrated her diamond jubilee with the people of Britain and the Commonwealth firmly behind them.

Above: Prince Philip with his grandsons, the Princes William and Harry, his son Prince Charles and Princess Diana's brother, Charles Spencer, Earl Althorp, as they walk behind the Princess's funeral cortège in 1997.

A LONG AND HAPPY MARRIAGE

In November 2007, the Queen and Prince Philip celebrated their golden wedding – 50 years of marriage, most of it conducted in the knowledge that their every move was subject to scrutiny from the press and public worldwide.

The Queen grew up knowing that this was to be her lot: a life of privilege, maybe, but one of service and duty in return for that privilege. Philip had no such expectations. He had as much royal blood coursing through his veins as the Queen – they shared great-great-grandparents – but Philip's unsettled childhood meant he had learnt to be extraordinarily self-reliant, pushing himself to extremes and accepting no boundaries in what was or was not possible.

Philip and Elizabeth were two quite separate characters bound by their fierce loyalty to each other and their love which deepened over the years. Because she is Queen, Philip is one of the few people who could talk to her and reassure her as one ordinary mortal to another. And because Philip can, at times, be grumpy and overbearing, she is able to tell him to behave himself – something no one else can do.

Her character is steadfast and quite stubborn. When, as a child of 13 years old, she fell in love with her handsome cousin who was showing off to please two young girls, she knew that this was the real thing. Her affection did not waver over the years. His grew more slowly but once he fell in love with 'Lilibet', he displayed the same loyalty and understanding.

Philip has been a moderniser, an action man who does not suffer fools gladly. He is also kind and compassionate, championing the underdog if he senses rudeness, injustice or foul play. When he was a young child, staying with the Foufounis family, fellow Greek émigrés, he grew fond of their young daughter, Ria, who was in plaster and immobile for several years because of a bad fall. An insensitive guest brought toys for all the children, except Ria, explaining that she was excluded because she could not play like the others. Philip ran out of the room and returned with his new gift and an armful of his old toys, which he placed on Ria's bed, saying, 'These are all for you!'

The Queen keeps her feelings tightly under control. She is unwavering in her duty, is exceptionally well-informed, because she works hard to be so, and rarely shows emotion. The exception was 1992, when she was visibly upset as she spoke of her 'annus horribilis' –

Below: A happy occasion: the Queen smiles as she and Philip celebrate their Golden Wedding anniversary with family members at a Westminster Abbey service of thanksgiving in 1997.

her 'horrible year' – when her beloved Windsor Castle was ravaged by fire and family problems were at the forefront of her mind. They stood together then as they always did, and both knew that she could not have carried out her daily duties without him providing loyal support and an arm to lean on at the end of the day. He knew that Elizabeth understood him well enough to give him the respect and freedom he needed to follow his own interests, including sailing, polo-playing and carriage driving. The couple must have hoped for more than just four years of comparatively normal married life before Elizabeth became Queen. But both were strong enough to sublimate their own wishes to the heavy responsibility of sovereignty.

Philip and Queen Elizabeth have formed a long and enduring partnership, privately and publicly, for over 70 years. With characteristic bluntness Philip used the term coined by his father-in-law, King George VI, to describe the royal hierarchy: the senior members are known as 'The Firm' and, as such, they work for Britain and the Commonwealth, at home and abroad. 'The Firm' comprises their four children: the heir to the throne, Prince Charles; the Princess Royal, Princess Anne; and Princes Andrew and Edward. They, with their partners, follow royal tradition of service as do the three younger members, the Duke and Duchess of Cambridge and Prince Harry, who have enthusiastically taken on the responsibility of many visits, patronages and charitable initiatives.

Above left: Detail from a stained-glass window based on a design by the Duke of Edinburgh. It was fitted in the restored Royal Chapel at Windsor Castle following the fire there in 1992 – the year the Queen termed her *'annus horribilis'*.

Above: Philip gallantly escorts his mother-in-law, the Queen Mother, as she arrives at Epsom racecourse in 2000, two months before her 100th birthday.

Above: The christening of Prince Philip's great-grandson, Prince George of Cambridge, at St James's Palace, 23 October 2013. Flanking Prince George and his mother, the Duchess of Cambridge, are his father, Prince William, and great-grandmother, Her Majesty The Queen. Standing (left to right) are: Prince Philip; the Prince of Wales and the Duchess of Cornwall; Prince Harry; Pippa and James Middleton; Carole and Michael Middleton.

Philip has watched his children grow up, has taught them to sail, ride and fish, and enjoy the simple pleasures of an outdoor life. He has stood with the Queen at the baptisms and the weddings of their children, watched milestones in their lives, such as when the Queen invested Prince Charles as Prince of Wales in Caernarfon Castle in 1969, and he applauded Princess Anne in 1976 when she won a place in the British Olympic Equestrian Team. He shared in the joy of the royal family and the nation as a whole when in 2011 his grandson, Prince William, married commoner Catherine Middleton in a ceremony with a light touch and comparative informality that delighted the world. The arrival of great-grandchildren, not least of all Prince George, fourth in line to the throne, has further enriched his life in later years.

The partnership between Philip and his wife, the Queen, was seen for the strong union it is during the year-long celebrations of her diamond jubilee – the 60 years of her reign that Philip has shared as consort and husband. Her Majesty has never hidden the extent of her reliance on Philip, the man she has called: 'My strength and stay all these years.' She is quoted as saying: 'I and his whole family, and this and many other countries, owe him a debt greater than he would ever claim or we shall ever know.'

It was apparent to many in the early days of their marriage, when they embarked on what was to become a lifetime's programme of visits and engagements, that Philip was more outgoing and less reserved than the then Princess Elizabeth. His self-reliance and ability to talk to people from all walks of life took the pressure from the young princess, still finding her way. By the time Elizabeth became queen, she was as adept as her husband at meeting people and putting them at their ease and together they made a formidable team for more than half a century.

Philip, 91 at the time of the diamond jubilee celebrations, was at the Queen's side as they travelled the length and breadth of the country, chatting to the great and the good and the general public alike. People turned out in their thousands to show their appreciation of the now elderly couple who were still carrying out many public engagements, performing their ceremonial duties, taking part in innumerable church services, shaking hands, sometimes with hundreds of people each day, eating many lunches and dinners with strangers and somehow always managing to smile and look interested and engaged.

Philip's absence, because of illness, over part of the main jubilee weekend jolted many into realising the enormous part he has played on these occasions. Without him, the Queen, although surrounded by her family and outwardly coping perfectly, must have felt alone, despite never showing it. Reticence is a royal virtue practised expertly by the most senior members of 'The Firm'.

Left: As smart and dutiful as ever in his 90s: Prince Philip, wearing uniform and medals, prepares to greet the President of the United Arab Emirates who arrived on a state visit to the UK in April 2013.

A LIFE OF SERVICE

In 1953, when Her Majesty was crowned, her husband and consort dedicated himself to her service, becoming her 'liege man of life and limb'. He was as good as his word and has given his whole life.

But his own list of innovations, achievements, service appointments, initiatives and patronages is immense. In 1947, the year of his marriage, he became patron of the London Federation of Boys' Clubs, an organisation which flourishes still as London Youth. That was the first of more than 800 associations and charities to which he has given his support.

Design was long a passion of his and in 1959 he set up several awards for design, technical industrial, artistic and general. He imitated the Prince Philip Medal for outstanding achievement in work with science or technology, and the President's Prize for Design Management at the Royal Society of Arts. The Duke of Edinburgh Award Scheme for young people is known the world over, while his interest in outdoor pursuits and service was reflected in his patronage of the Outward Bound Trust and the British Association for Shooting and Conservation, Voluntary Service Overseas and the Dawn to Dusk flying competition for the Duke of Edinburgh trophy. These are just a few of the hundreds of initiatives and organisations he has backed. In addition he has travelled the world, promoting British business and technology.

Right: Navy days are recalled in 1995 as the Duke chats to old shipmates who served with him on HMS *Whelp* during the Second World War.

As well as holding many service appointments in the Army, Navy and Air Force, he was an outstanding polo player as a young man, and went on to represent his country at the Four-in-Hand World (carriage) Driving Championships on many occasions. He wrote several books on carriage driving and on conservation.

Philip is the longest-serving royal consort in British history but he and the Queen are equal partners in their life of service to their country. In this they sustain each other, allowing Elizabeth to rule with grace and equanimity and Philip, the once rootless boy, to achieve the respect of a nation.

Right: Young people enjoy the Duke's company at a reception to celebrate the 500th Duke of Edinburgh Awards presentation in October 2013.

REFLECTIONS ON A LONG CAREER

On 9 September 2015, Her Majesty the Queen became the longest-reigning British monarch, having served her country dutifully and with devotion for 63 years. In doing so, she has surpassed the record set by her own great-grandmother Queen Victoria, the two queens being the only British monarchs in history to celebrate their diamond jubilees. Since then, she has served a further two years and, on 13 October 2016, the same year in which she marked her sapphire jubilee of 65 years on the throne and following the death of Thailand's Bhumibol Aduladej, she became the world's longest-reigning surviving monarch.

Throughout these many decades there has been one constant by her side, her beloved Philip, the Duke of Edinburgh. After a similarly long career– initially in the Navy and thereafter as royal consort – at the age of 96, Philip took the decision to bow out of public life and take a well-earned retirement, a decision taken with the full support of the Queen and other senior members of the royal family.

His presence, support and companionship during state visits and other official engagements undertaken by Her Majesty will undoubtedly be sorely missed, but after tens of thousands of engagements, of which more than 22,000 have been solo, and nearly 5,500 speeches, the Duke felt it was time to take life at a more leisurely pace and perhaps have a little more time to devote to his interests, which still include carriage driving, painting and outdoor pursuits.

However, he has promised that he won't disappear from the public eye completely. He will continue with his support for the many organisations – numbering in excess of 700 – that have him as a member, president or patron and he will also follow the further development of the Duke of Edinburgh Award Scheme that to date has benefited more than five million young people. He has affirmed that, in addition, he will from time to time, accept invitations for certain events, but in the future these will be those of his own choosing, which tie in with his personal interests.

Despite being of royal blood, Prince Philip did not have the easiest start in life, experiencing loss, heartache and instability in his young years, but thanks to his indomitable spirit and leadership qualities, both of which were honed at Gordonstoun and in the Navy, he was able to put his early troubles behind him to follow a successful career as 'second-in-command' to his wife, tailoring his work to satisfy his personal needs and all the while remaining his own man.

Upon his marriage, the Duke was fully aware of the duties that lay ahead of him and was ready and willing to take them on, but even he could never have envisaged back then that these duties might go on for more than six decades. Nevertheless, over that time, he gave the country his unstinted support without question nor resentment, to become, as he has put it in his own inimitable way, 'the world's most experience plaque unveiler', a modest statement that belies the achievements of this truly remarkable man.

Right: The Duke of Edinburgh at the Menin Gate memorial in Belgium where he led tributes to fallen troops.

Back cover: Queen Elizabeth II and the Duke of Edinburgh gaze lovingly at each other at Broadlands in 2017.